A JOKE-A-DAY:

200 Kid-Friendly Jokes For The Classroom

ppy, smiling children make for eager, engaged learners. With the
riad of testing and assessments that take place throughout the
hool year, it is nice to have a moment each day to make kids
ile. Whether you start the morning off with a joke or fit it in
tween math and reading lessons, a kid-friendly joke, tongue
ister, or riddle helps lighten the mood and gets your students
inking outside the box.

kes and riddles offer a great segue into multiple word meanings,
mophones, language manipulation, alliteration, and more. Need
new way to grab your ESL/ELL students' attention? Try telling
em a joke. Want to challenge your students to use language in
fferent ways? Ask them to write jokes and riddles. The inherent
un factor" of jokes makes them an easy sell and much less
timidating than asking students to write a paragraph.

you think writing a joke is easy, think again. It requires
udents to not only understand the way words are put together,
t encourages them to expand their vocabulary. With a strong
phasis in the Common Core State Standards on vocabulary,
riting and telling jokes is the perfect, kid-friendly way to meet
ose standards.

e 200 kid-friendly jokes in this book are great for classroom
r home) use. Encourage students to create a joke a day for your
assroom and create a book that they can take home at the end
the year. Inspiration, humor, and kid-friendly fun are a
re-fire recipe for student success.

this book belongs to

Q: What do you get when you throw a lot of books into the ocean?

A: A title wave.

Q: What has four wheels and flies?

A: A trash truck.

Q: Why couldn't the bicycle stand up?

A: Because it was two tired.

Q: What do you call a boomerang that doesn't come back?

A: A stick.

Q: Why did the chicken go to jail?

A: Because he was using fowl language.

Q: What has two legs but can't walk?

A: A pair of pants

Q: Why was the math book always worried?

A: Because it had so many problems.

Q: Which school supply is king of the classroom?

A: The ruler

Q: Which vegetable should you never invite on a boat trip?

A: A leek.

Q: How did Benjamin Franklin feel when he discovered electricity?

A: He was shocked.

Q: Why did the horse chew with his mouth open?

A: Because he had bad stable manners.

Q: What's a tornado's favorite game to play?

A: Twister

Q: What do you give a sick lemon?

A: Lemon-aid.

Q: What did the mouse say to the
other mouse when he tried to steal his
cheese?

A: That's nacho cheese.

Q: Why couldn't the pirate play cards?

A: Because he was always on the deck.

Q: Where do polar bears vote?

A: At the North Pole.

Q: What's a ghost's favorite fruit?

A: Boo-berries.

Q: Why did the robber take a shower?

A: Because he wanted to make a clean getaway

Q: What did the mayonnaise say when the refrigerator was opened?

A: Close the door! I'm dressing!

Q: What do you call a shoe made from a banana?

A: A slipper.

Q: What did the apple tree say to the farmer?

A: Stop picking on me!

Q: Why are there fences around cemeteries?

A: Because people are dying to get in

Q: Where do cows go on the weekend?

A: To the moo-vies.

Q: Why did the pony get detention?

A: Because he was horsing around.

Q: What lights up a stadium?

A: A soccer match.

Q: What's bigger than an elephant, but doesn't weigh anything?

A: His shadow.

Q: Why did the teacher have to wear
sunglasses?

A: Because her students were so bright.

Q: Which bus crossed the ocean?

A: Columbus.

Q: What do you call a pig that does karate?

A: A pork chop

Q: Why was six afraid of seven?

A: Because seven eight nine.

Q: What do you call a fish with no eye?

A: A fsh.

Q: What do gymnasts, acrobats, and bananas all have in common?

A: They can all do splits.

Q: What's a frog's favorite game?

A: Hopscotch

Q: What dies but never lives?

A: A battery

Q: What day of the week does the potato look forward to the least?

A: Fry-day

Q: What do you call a seagull that flies over the bay?

A: A bagel.

Q: What is Dracula's
favorite fruit?

A: Neck-tarines.

Q: What does a skeleton
order for dinner?

A: Spare ribs.

Q: What's a ghost's
favorite dessert?

A: Ice Scream.

Q: How do monsters tell their
fortunes?

A: They read their horror-scopes

Q: Where does the witch park her vehicle?

A: In the broom closet.

Q: What is a witch's favorite subject in school?

A: Spelling.

Q: Why couldn't the ghost see his parents?

A: Because they were trans-parents.

Q: What do you do if you're a fan of Dracula's?

A: You join his fang club.

Q: Where do ghosts go for a
swim?

A: The Dead Sea.

Q: Whom did the monster
ask to kiss his boo-boos
after he fell?

A: His mummy

Q: What makes a skeleton
laugh?

A: When something tickles his
funny bone.

Q: What would you get if you crossed a
teacher with a vampire?

A: Lots of blood tests.

Q: Why did the Cyclops stop teaching?

A: Because he only had one pupil.

Q: Why didn't Dracula have any friends?

A: Because he was a pain in the neck.

Q: Where did the witch have to go
when she misbehaved?

A: To her broom.

Q: What do you get if you cross a
vampire and a snowman?

A: Frostbite.

Q: What's a ghost's favorite room in the house?

A: The living room.

Q: What do birds do on Halloween?

A: They go trick or tweeting.

Q: What's a ghost's favorite room in
the house?

A: The living room.

Q: Which monster is the best dance
partner?

A: The Boogie Man.

Q: What did the turkey stay before it
was roasted?

A: I'm stuffed!

Q: Why was the turkey arrested?

A: It was suspected of fowl play.

Q: What smells the best at
Thanksgiving?

A: Your nose.

Q: What kind of weather does a turkey
like?

A: Fowl weather.

Q: What always comes at the end of Thanksgiving?

A: The letter "g."

Q: What kind of weather does a turkey like?

A: Fowl weather.

Q: Why couldn't the turkey eat dessert?

A: Because he was stuffed

Q: What type of key is the most important at Thanksgiving dinner?

A: The tur-key

Q: Why couldn't the turkey eat dessert?

A: Because he was stuffed

Q: What type of key is the most important at Thanksgiving dinner?

A: The tur-key

Q: Which side of the turkey has the
most feathers?

A: The outside.

Q: Are turkey leftovers good for your
health?

A: Not if you're the turkey

Q: What do elves learn in school?

A: The elf-abet.

Q: What do you get if you cross a pine tree with an apple?

A: A pine-apple.

Q: What type of diet did the snowman
go on?

A: The Meltdown Diet.

Q: What did the snowman have for
breakfast?

A: Frosted Flakes

Q: What do you have in December that
you don't have in any other month?

A: The letter "d."

Q: What often falls in winter, but
never gets hurt?

A: Snow.

Q: Why did the boy keep his trumpet in
the freezer?

A: Because he liked cool music.

Q: What's brown and sneaks around
the kitchen?

A: Mince spies.

Q: What's the difference between a Christmas alphabet and the regular alphabet?

A: The Christmas alphabet has Noel.

Q: What happened to the man who stole a calendar from the store?

A: He got 12 months.

Q: Why was Santa's helper sad?

A: Because he had low elf-esteem.

Q: What does Santa clean his sleigh with?

A: Comet.

Q: Why was Santa's helper sad?

A: Because he had low elf-esteem.

Q: What does Santa clean his sleigh
with?

A: Comet.

Q: What did the stamp say to the
envelope?

A: I'm stuck on you.

Q: What did the paper clip say to the
magnet?

A: I find you very attractive.

Q: What kind of flower do you never want to get on Valentine's Day?

A: Cauliflower.

Q: What do elephants say to one another on Valentine's Day?

A: I love you a ton.

Q: What's easy to get into, but hard to get out of?

A: Trouble.

Q: Why is the forest so noisy?

A: Because the trees have bark.

Knock, knock.

Who's there?

Wet.

Wet who?

Wet me in, it's raining out here!

Q: If a butcher wears a size XL shirt and a size 13 shoe, what does he weigh?

A: Meat.

Q: What did the baker say to his wife?

A: I'm dough-nuts about you

Q: What did the squirrel give for Valentine's Day?

A: Forget-me-nuts.

Q: What do you call two birds in love?

Who's there?

Arthur

Arthur who?

Arthur anymore chocolates left?

Q: What did the monster ask his sweetheart?

A: Will you be my Valen-slime?

Q: What did the boy pickle say to the
girl pickle?

A: You mean a great dill to me.

Q: What did the farmer give his wife
for Valentine's Day?

A: Hogs and kisses.

Q: What did the owl say to his
sweetheart?

A: Owl be yours.

Q: What did the calculator say to the
other calculator on Valentine's Day?

A: Let me count the ways I love you.

Q: What did one piece of string say to
the other piece of string?

A: Will you be my Valen-twine?

Q: Why did the boy bring a ladder to
school?

A: He wanted to go to high school.

Q: What are there a lot of when
turkeys play baseball?

A: Fowl balls

Q: Where do pencils go for vacation?

A: Pencil-vania.

Q: What did the snowman order at Wendy's®?

A: A Frosty!

Q: Why can't skeletons play music?

A: Because they have no organs.

Q: How do you catch an unusual rabbit?

A: Unique up on it.

Q: What's the best way to talk to a T-Rex?

A: From a distance.

Q: What kind of music do mummies
like best?

A: Wrap.

Q: Why did the elephant cross the road?

A: Because it was the chicken's day off.

Q: Where can you learn to make ice cream?

A: At Sundae School.

Q: Why did the boy run around his bed?

A: He was trying to catch up on his sleep.

Q: What do you call an elephant in a
phone booth?

A: Stuck!

Q: How does the Easter Bunny travel?

A: By hare-plane.

Q: What runs but never walks?

A: A hose.

Q: Which flower talks the most?

A: Tulips, because they have two lips.

Q: What did the spoon say to the knife?

A: "You're so sharp!"

Q: How did the hairdresser win the race?

A: She knew a shortcut.

Q: Why are fish so smart?

A: Because they are always in a school.

Q: What did the dinner plate say to the cup?

A: Dinner's on me tonight.

Q: What did the circle say to the
triangle?

A: I don't see your point.

Q: What's black and white over and
over again?

A: A penguin rolling down a hill.

Q: What's a rabbit's favorite kind of
music?

A: Hip-hop.

Q: Where's a wall's favorite place to
meet his friends?

A: At the corner.

Q: Where did the king keep his army?

A: In his sleeve.

Q: Why don't animals eat clowns?

A: They taste funny!

Q: Where do books hide when they're scared?

A: Under their covers.

Q: What's a scarecrow's favorite fruit?

A: Strawberries.

Q: Why can't the elephant use the computer?

A: Because he's afraid of the mouse.

Knock, knock.

Who's there?

Who.

Who who?

Is there an owl in here?

Q: What do ghosts use to wash their
hair?

A: Sham-BOO.

Q: What did the carrot say to the
mushroom?

A: You're a fungi (fun guy).

Q: What did the hamburger name her
daughter?

A: Patty.

Q: What do a car and an elephant have
in common?

A: They both have trunks.

Knock, knock.

Who's there?

Tank.

Tank who?

You're welcome!

Q: Why do cowboys ride horses?

A: Because they're too heavy to carry.

Q: What is a math teacher's favorite
type of dessert?

A: Pi.

Q: Why was the cafeteria clock always
behind?

A: Because it went back for seconds.

Q: Why is 1+1=3 like your left foot?

A: It's not right.

Q: Where do kids in New York City
learn multiplication?

A: In Times Square.

Q: Why did everyone want the music teacher to be on their baseball team?

A: Because she had the perfect pitch.

Q: Why are elephants such bad dancers?

A: Because they have two left feet.

Q: What starts and ends with "e" and
only has one letter?

A: An envelope.

Knock, knock.

Who's there?

Cows go.

Cows go who?

No, silly, cows go MOO!

Q: What's a math teacher's favorite
tool?

A: Multipliers.

Q: What should you do if your teacher
rolls her eyes at you?

A: Roll them back, of course!

Q: Why do bees have sticky hair?

A: Because they have honeycombs.

Knock, knock.

Who's there?

Cash.

Cash who?

No, thanks, I prefer peanuts.

Q: Why didn't the oven go to college?

A: Because it had a lot of degrees already.

Knock, knock.

Who's there?

Pecan.

Pecan who?

Pecan someone your own size!

Q: What did the teacher do at the beach?

A: She tested the water.

Q: What time is it when you have a toothache?

A: Tooth Hurty.

Q: How did the boy react when his
turtle died?

A: He was shell-shocked.

Q: What's a spider's favorite thing to
do on a computer?

A: Make websites.

Q: What kind of table can you have for
dinner?

A: A vege-table.

Q: What's a librarian's favorite type of
bait when fishing?

A: Bookworms.

Q: What did one eye say to the other?

A: Between you and I, something smells.

Q: Why did the girl put lipstick on her head?

A: Because she wanted to make-up her mind

Q: What's a cannibal's favorite sport?

A: Football.

Q: What did the ocean say to the beach?

A: Nothing, it just waved.

Q: What do you call a worm with no
teeth?

A: A gummy worm.

Q: Why was the computer cold?

A: Because it left the Windows open!

Q: What did the doctor diagnose the horse with when he wasn't feeling well?

A: Hay fever.

Q: Why do birds fly south for the winter?

A: Because it's too far to walk.

Q: What lies at the bottom of the
ocean and worries?

A: A nervous wreck.

Knock, knock.

Who's there?

Nobel.

Nobel who?

There's nobel, that's why I'm knocking.

Q: What's the smartest insect around?

A: The spelling bee.

Q: Why did the cabbage beat the carrot in a race?

A: Because it was a-head.

Q: Why don't ducks tell jokes when they fly?

A: They would quack up!

Knock, knock.

Who's there?

Leaf.

Leaf who?

Leaf me alone please, I'm thinking.

Q: What's a bat's favorite pastime?

A: Hanging out with his friends.

Q: Where do polar bears keep their money?

A: In snow banks.

Q: How do bears keep their den cool in
the summer?

A: They use bear-conditioning.

Knock, knock.

Who's there?

Canoe.

Canoe who?

Canoe help me with my homework
please?

Q: Why was the clown crying?

A: Because he broke his funny bone.

Q: What did the paper say to
encourage the pencil?

A: Write on, good friend!

Q: Where can you always find a
peacock?

A: In the dictionary.

Q: What is a top's favorite ride at the
amusement park?

A: The merry-go-round.

Q: What is a kitten's favorite dessert?

A: Mice cream.

Q: Where did the bird go when he lost a feather?

A: The re-tail shop.

Q: What's a cat's favorite nursery
rhyme?

A: Three Blind Mice.

Q: Why did the dog keep tripping?

A: Because she had two left feet.

Q: What did the duck say to the clown?

A: You quack me up!

Knock, knock.

Who's there?

Nana.

Nana who?

Nana your business.

Q: Where do baby pens spend their day?

A: In their play pen.

Q: What has 18 legs and catches flies?

A: A baseball team.

Q: Why is it not a good idea to try to trick a snake?

A: Because you can't pull his leg.

Knock, knock.

Who's there?

Needle.

Needle who?

Needle little more money for this toy please.

Q: What was the banker's favorite
player on the football team?

A: The quarterback.

Knock, knock.

Who's there?

Yukon.

Yukon who?

Yukon a let us in? It's raining out here!

Q: What bird loves construction work?

A: A crane.

Q: Why couldn't the boy go to the
pirate movie?

A: Because it was rated "ARRR!"

Q: What did the farmer say to the horse when he walked in the barn?

A: "Why the long face?"

Q: How long should an elephant's legs be?

A: Long enough to reach the ground.

Q: What do you call a left-handed dog?

A: A south paw.

Q: What gives you the power to walk
through a wall?

A: A door.

Q: Why did the book join the police force?

A: He wanted to go undercover.

Q: What did the students do when their shoelaces got tangled together?

A: They went on a class trip

www.ingramcontent.com/pod-product-compliance
Lightning Source LLC
Chambersburg PA
CBHW081351160726
48000CB00010B/3300